A Robbie Reader

Dakota Fanning

Joanne Mattern

P.O. Box 196
Hockessin, Delaware 19707
Visit us on the web: www.mitchelllane.com
Comments? email us: mitchelllane@mitchelllane.com

Mitchell Lane PUBLISHERS

Printing   1   2   3   4   5   6   7   8   9

A Robbie Reader
Contemporary Biography

Alex Rodriguez	Brittany Murphy	Charles Schulz
Dakota Fanning	Dale Earnhardt Jr.	Donovan McNabb
Dr. Seuss	Hilary Duff	Jamie Lynn Spears
Jesse McCartney	Johnny Gruelle	LeBron James
Mia Hamm	Shaquille O'Neal	The Story of Harley-Davidson
Syd Hoff	Tiki Barber	Tony Hawk

Library of Congress Cataloging-in-Publication Data
Mattern, Joanne, 1963–
    Dakota Fanning / by Joanne Mattern.
        p. cm. – (A Robbie reader)
    Includes bibliographical references and index.
    ISBN 1-58415-519-1 (lib. bound)
    1. Fanning, Dakota, 1994– —Juvenile literature. 2. Actors—United States—
Biography—Juvenile literature. I. Title. II. Series.
PN2287.F325M38 2006
791.4302'8092—dc22
                                                                        2006006113

ISBN-10: 1-58415-519-1   ISBN-13: 9781584155195

ABOUT THE AUTHOR: Joanne Mattern is the author of more than 100 nonfiction books for children. Along with biographies, she has written extensively about animals, nature, history, sports, and foreign cultures. She wrote *Brian McBride, Peyton Manning, Miguel Tejada,* and *Tiki Barber* for Mitchell Lane Publishers. She lives near New York City with her husband and three young daughters.

PHOTO CREDITS: Cover, Frank Micelotta/Getty Images; pp. 4, 24—Kevin Winter/ Getty Images; p. 6—AFP/AFP/Getty Images; p. 8—Frazer Harrison/Getty Images; p. 22—Vince Bucci; p. 10—Nina Prommer/Globe Photos; p. 12—Stuart Ramson/ AP Photo, p. 14—Sebastian Artz/Getty Images; pp. 16, 19, 20, 21, 27—Globe Photos; p. 25—Michael Buckner/Getty Images.

PLB

TABLE OF CONTENTS

Dakota Fanning is all smiles as she accepts the Best Young Actress award at the 11th Annual Critics' Choice Awards. At only 11 years old, she had already received several acting awards.

And the Winner Is . . . Dakota!

In 2002, eight-year-old Dakota Fanning sat in the audience at the Broadcast Film Critics Association Awards. She was the youngest person in the room. Even though she was just a little girl, she was there for a big reason. She had acted in a movie called *I Am Sam*. She had been **nominated** for the Best Young Actor **award**.

Other actors had also been nominated. One was Daniel Radcliffe, the star of the popular Harry Potter movies. Another was Haley Joel Osment, who had been in the movie *AI: Artificial Intelligence*.

Dakota played the part of Lucy in the movie *I Am Sam*. The role made eight-year-old Dakota a star.

Finally, the award for the Best Young Actor was announced. The winner was . . . Dakota Fanning!

A happy Dakota went up to the stage to get her award. Then she turned to make a speech. There was just one problem. She was too short to reach the microphone.

An actor named Orlando Bloom was standing next to the microphone. He came to Dakota's rescue. Orlando picked her up and held her close to the microphone while she gave her speech. She thanked the many people who had helped her become an actress.

By 2002, Dakota was a winner in many ways. She was a movie star. She was also an ordinary, happy little girl.

Dakota (left) and her sister, Elle, attend the 12th Annual Dream Halloween Fundraiser. They are holding Polly Pocket dolls that were made to look like them.

Birth of a Star

Hannah Dakota Fanning was born on February 23, 1994, in Conyers, Georgia. Dakota's mother is Joy. Her father is Steven. Steve Fanning used to be a minor-league baseball player. When Dakota was born, he worked for an electrical business. Dakota has a younger sister named Elle.

Very early in Dakota's life, her parents saw that she was special. When she was two years old, she had already learned how to read. Joy Fanning thought that Dakota might like acting. She signed her up for acting classes.

Being an actress is hard work. Dakota had to learn and remember lines. She had to pretend to be someone else. She had to show

Dakota (left) and Elle attend the opening of Dakota's movie *Dreamer.*

her character's feelings to the audience. Acting coaches helped her learn how to do all these things.

Dakota loved acting. "I love to pretend," she says.

Dakota's coaches loved her too. They told her parents that she was very **talented**. They suggested that Dakota get an **agent** so that she could get paid for acting.

Dakota's parents agreed. They found an agent for her in Georgia.

It did not take long for Dakota to get her first role. In 1999, she was in a television commercial for Tide laundry detergent. Dakota was just five years old.

Dakota's agent told the Fannings they should move to Los Angeles, California, where many television shows and movies are taped. If Dakota lived in Los Angeles, she could try out for acting roles there.

Moving to Los Angeles would be a big change. The Fannings knew Dakota loved acting. They knew she could be a star. But they weren't sure about leaving Georgia.

Finally, the Fannings decided to go. In January 2000, Dakota and her family moved to California. No one knew it yet, but Dakota's acting career was about to take off.

Dakota poses with the Muppets at the Entertainment Industry Foundation's musical benefit, which raises money for cancer research.

TV Times

The Fanning family did not think they would stay in Los Angeles for a long time. "It was supposed to be for six weeks," her mother said. However, things turned out very differently.

In April 2000, Dakota got her first big role on television. She played a patient on the hit TV show *ER*. The show takes place in the emergency room of a hospital.

Six-year-old Dakota loved the experience. "I played a car accident victim," she said. "I got to wear a neck brace and nose tubes for the two days I worked."

Many more interesting roles followed. Dakota appeared on another popular show

Dakota attends the **premiere** of the Disney film *Snow Dogs* in 2002. She enjoys going to movie premieres, even if she did not act in the movie.

Dakota's beauty and acting skills have made her a star.

called *Ally McBeal.* She played Ally as a young girl. In 2000, she also appeared in other hit TV shows. She was in *CSI, The Practice,* and *Spin City.*

Dakota continued acting on television in 2001. Most of the time, she was a guest star. Other times, only her voice was heard. In November, Dakota provided the voice of a little girl in the cartoon *Family Guy.*

Dakota had become a popular television actress by 2001. However, her career was about to take another leap. It was time for Dakota to appear in the movies.

Brittany Murphy and Dakota Fanning starred in the 2003 movie *Uptown Girls.*

Making Movies

Dakota's part in her first movie, called *Tomcats,* was very small. Her role was the little girl in the park. Dakota had fun making the movie, which came out in 2001. She enjoyed working with other actors.

In 2001, seven-year-old Dakota took on her biggest role yet. She played a girl named Lucy in the movie *I Am Sam.* The movie also starred Sean Penn, who played Lucy's father, Sam. The courts try to take Lucy away from Sam. They say that Sam cannot raise Lucy because he is **disabled**. Sam must fight to keep Lucy with him.

Everyone on the set enjoyed working with Dakota. Jessie Nelson, the director of the film, said, "Dakota possesses a real strength and wisdom that is beyond her years." Dakota also became friends with Sean Penn.

Dakota received a lot of praise for her acting in *I Am Sam*. One reviewer said that she was "an absolute angel with smarts."

In 2002, a group called the Screen Actors Guild (SAG) nominated several people as Best Supporting Actress of the year. One of them was Dakota Fanning. At only eight years old, she was the youngest person to be nominated for a SAG award.

Dakota told reporters that she was sleeping in her mother's bed when she heard the news. "I jumped on the bed, but my mother's bed is really, really big," she said. "I was afraid I was going to hit my head because I was jumping so high."

Dakota did not win the SAG award. Still, her acting in *I Am Sam* made her a star.

Dakota made many more movies between 2001 and 2005. In 2002, she appeared in

Dakota cuddles with actor Sean Penn in a scene from their movie, *I Am Sam.*

Taken, a TV miniseries by executive producer Steven Spielberg. She worked with Spielberg again in 2005 for *War of the Worlds.*

Dakota's most popular movies were *Uptown Girls* (2003), *The Cat in the Hat* (2003), *Man on Fire* (2004), *War of the Worlds* (2005), and *Dreamer: Inspired by a True Story* (2005). She has appeared onscreen with some of the most famous actors in Hollywood.

Dakota with her costars Spencer Breslin (left) and Mike Myers (center) in a scene from the movie *The Cat in the Hat*.

Dakota also continued doing cartoon voices. In 2003, she did the voice of a young Kim Possible in the TV movie *Kim Possible: A Stitch in Time*. She also did the voice of Lilo in the video *Lilo & Stitch 2: Stitch Has a Glitch*.

Dakota loves making movies. In 2003, Dakota told *Newsweek* magazine, "When I'm not working I'm like, 'Oh, I wish I could be on

Dakota Fanning and Tom Cruise appear in a scene from the 2005 movie *War of the Worlds.*

the set now.' " In another interview for *People* magazine, Dakota said the hardest part of making a movie was finishing the job. "You get to know everybody for so long, and then you have to say goodbye." She really misses the friends she makes on her movie sets.

In 2005, Dakota was honored for being a positive role model for young people at the Rising Stars 50th Anniversary Gala.

A Regular Girl

Dakota Fanning lives a very different life than most other children. Yet in many ways she is just like any other young girl. Dakota's favorite hobby is reading. She takes a book with her wherever she goes.

Dakota also treasures the time she spends with her little sister, Elle. "We play Barbie and dress up," Dakota told *People* magazine in 2003. That same year, she told *Time for Kids* about other favorite hobbies. "I just learned how to play the piano. I'm really excited about that. I love that. I love my knitting. I love to read. Those are pretty much the things that I do."

Being a movie star is a fun way for Dakota to play dress-up. She wears costumes in her movies and fancy dresses to movie premieres. Dakota loves these dresses. "I never want to take them off," she told *People* magazine.

In 2005, Dakota starred in the movie *Dreamer*, which is about a girl and her horse. She had never ridden a horse before she made the movie. However, she fell in love with the animals. She was very happy when her costar, Kurt Russell, bought a horse for her when the

Dakota and costar Kurt Russell arrive in style at the premiere of their movie, *Dreamer*.

filming was over. Making *Dreamer* also made Dakota want to help horses. She began working with a charity that helps save **endangered** wild horses.

Dakota does not go to a regular school. Instead, she is home-schooled. However, she likes to spend time with other girls her age. In 2005, she became a member of a Girl Scout troop in California. "I'm really excited to get to sell the cookies," she told *People* magazine. "I've always wanted to do that!"

In 2005, Dakota and her Girl Scout troop attended a special screening of *Dreamer*.

In 2006, twelve-year-old Dakota took on two very different roles. She played Fern in *Charlotte's Web*. This movie is based on a popular children's book. Dakota also took on a more adult role in the movie *Hounddog*. In this movie, her character copes with horrible events by listening to the music of Elvis Presley.

Dakota's parents make sure she has the chance to be a regular kid. They do not let her go to parties. They make sure no one takes photographs of the family when they are spending private time together. In 2005, a comedian named Kathy Griffin joked that Dakota had a problem with drugs. Griffin was just kidding. However, Dakota's family and friends got very angry. Finally, the **network** that had broadcast Griffin's joke apologized.

The Fannings still have a home in Georgia. The family returns there whenever they can. Dakota treasures the time she spends with family and friends in her home state. "All my happy memories are in Georgia," Dakota told an Atlanta magazine. "And you can bet I have lots of them."

Dakota enjoys acting with animals. In *Charlotte's Web*, she worked with Wilbur the pig.

Dakota Fanning has a life most other people cannot imagine. She has met and worked with some of Hollywood's brightest stars. However, she is still a fun-loving young girl. She enjoys most of the same things other children her age do. Dakota has a talent for acting. She also has a talent for making every part of her life special.

CHRONOLOGY

1994   Hannah Dakota Fanning is born in Conyers, Georgia, on February 23.

1996   Dakota teachers herself how to read.

1999   Dakota appears in a television commercial for Tide detergent.

2000   The Fannings move to Los Angeles; Dakota appears in her first TV show, *ER*; she also appears in *Ally McBeal, CSI, The Practice,* and *Spin City.*

2001   Dakota makes her movie debut in *Tomcats*; she stars in *I Am Sam.*

2002   Dakota becomes the youngest actress to be nominated for a Screen Actors Guild award. She wins the Broadcast Film Critics Association award for the Best Young Actor. She appears in *Sweet Home Alabama* with Reese Witherspoon.

2003   Dakota stars in the films *Uptown Girls* and *The Cat in the Hat*; she makes many television appearances.

2004   Dakota stars in *Man on Fire* with Denzel Washington.

2005   Dakota stars in *The War of the Worlds* with Tom Cruise and in *Dreamer* with Kurt Russell. She begins working with a charity whose aim is to save wild horses.

2006   Dakota plays Fern in *Charlotte's Web* and Lewellen in *Hounddog.*

2006   *Hounddog*

Charlotte's Web

2005   *Dreamer: Inspired by a True Story*

Lilo and Stitch 2: Stitch Has a Glitch

The War of the Worlds

Hide and Seek

2004   *Man on Fire*

2003   *The Cat in the Hat*

Uptown Girls

2002   *Taken*—TV miniseries

Sweet Home Alabama

2001   *I Am Sam*

Articles

Campeau, Melissa. "Down with DAKOTA." *Kids Tribute*, Fall 2005, volume 17, issue 3.

Carter, Kelly. " 'Sam' Brings Fame to Dakota." *USA Today*, March 6, 2002.

"Dakota Fanning." *Newsweek*, December 8, 2003, volume 142, issue 23.

El Nabli, Dina. "Dakota Fanning, Actress." *Time for Kids News*, December 1, 2003. http://www.timeforkids.com/TFK/news/story/0,6260,544728,00.html

"Sister Act." *People*, August 25, 2003, volume 60, issue 8.

Speight, Kimberly, and Rachel Fischer Spalding. "Ones to Watch." *Hollywood Reporter, International Edition*, November 20, 2001, volume 370, issue 49.

Valby, Karen. "The Most Powerful Actress in Hollywood Is . . . Dakota Fanning." *Entertainment Weekly*, July 29, 2005, issue 831.

On the Internet

Dakota Fanning
http://www.imdb.com/name/nm0266824
Dakota Fanning: Yahoo! Movies
http://movies.yahoo.com/shop?d=hc&id=1804501481&cf=gen
TV.com
http://tv.com/dakota-fanning/person/26659/summary.html

agent (AY-junt)—Someone who plans jobs for people.

award (uh-WARD)—A prize.

disabled (dis-AY-buld)—Refers to people who have either physical or mental impairments.

endangered (in-DAYN-jurd)—In danger of dying out completely.

network (NET-wurk)—A group of television stations.

nominated (NAH-muh-nay-tid)—Named as deserving of an honor or award.

premiere (preh-MEER)—The first public performance of a movie or play.

talent (TAA-lent)—A skill or ability to do something.

READ-ALOUD PROGRAM

JUNIOR GREAT BOOKS

DRAGON SERIES
VOLUME 1

The Great Books Foundation

A nonprofit educational corporation

15 14 13 12

Printed in the United States of America

Published and distributed by

THE GREAT BOOKS FOUNDATION

A nonprofit educational corporation

35 East Wacker Drive, Suite 400

Chicago, IL 60601

Note to the At-Home Reader

Read the assigned story aloud, making sure your child can see the text and pictures as you read. Ask your child to say the underlined phrases in the book with you. Whenever the character "G.B." (pictured above) appears, you will know that you should ask your child the question in the box. Give your child time to think through and talk over his or her answer. Whenever you can, ask your child **why** he or she gave that answer. Keep in mind that these are open-ended questions for which there are no single right answers. When G.B.'s question calls for an answer to be marked, help your child do so.

When you have finished the reading, ask your child what question he or she has about the story. Write this question on the lines provided at the end of the selection.

For the "Nature Speaks" poetry unit, read "Theme in Yellow" once through, asking your child to chorus the underlined phrases with you. Then read the poem a second time, discussing G.B.'s questions as they occur.

Your child will read and discuss the other two poems, "The Wind" and "Seashell," later, in class, but feel free to enjoy these poems together at any time.

The blank pages in this book are for activities that will be completed in class. Encourage your child to show you his or her work when each unit is finished.

THE
FROG
PRINCE

BROTHERS GRIMM

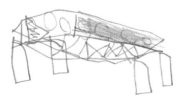

The hardest thing would be ___THE APOG AND the phippines___

In the olden days when wishing was still
of some use, there lived a King. He had several
beautiful daughters, but the youngest was so fair
that even the sun, who sees so many wonders,
could not help marveling every time
he looked into her face.

Near the King's palace lay a large dark forest and there, under an old linden tree, was a well. When the day was very warm, the little Princess would go off into this forest and sit at the rim of the cool well. There she would play with her golden ball, tossing it up and catching it deftly in her little hands. This was her favorite game and she never tired of it.

Now it happened one day that, as the Princess tossed her golden ball into the air, it did not fall into her uplifted hands as usual. Instead, it fell to the ground, rolled to the rim of the well and into the water. **Plunk, splash!** The golden ball was gone.

The well was deep and the Princess knew it. She felt sure she would never see her beautiful ball again, so she cried and cried and could not stop.

"What is the matter, little Princess?" said a voice behind her. "You are crying so that even a hard stone would have pity on you."

The little girl looked around and there she saw a frog. He was in the well and was stretching his fat ugly head out of the water.

"Oh, it's you—you old water-splasher!" said the girl. "I'm crying over my golden ball. It has fallen into the well."

"Oh, as to that," said the frog, "I can bring your ball back to you. But what will you give me if I do?"

"Whatever you wish, dear old frog," said the Princess. "I'll give you my dresses, my beads and all my jewelry—even the golden crown on my head."

The frog answered: "Your dresses, your beads and all your jewelry, even the golden crown on your head—I don't want them. But if you can find it in your heart to like me and take me for your playfellow, if you will let me sit beside you at the table, eat from your little golden plate and drink from your little golden cup, and if you are willing to let me sleep in your own little bed besides: if you promise me all this, little Princess, then I will gladly go down to the bottom of the well and bring back your golden ball."

"Oh yes," said the Princess, "I'll promise anything you say if you'll only bring back my golden ball to me." But to herself she thought: "What is the silly frog chattering about? He can only live in the water and croak with the other frogs; he could never be a playmate to a human being."

As soon as the frog had heard her
promise, he disappeared into the well.
Down, down, down, he sank; but he
soon came up again, holding the
golden ball in his mouth. He dropped
it on the grass at the feet of the Princess
who was wild with joy when she saw
her favorite plaything once more.
She picked up the ball and skipped
away with it, thinking no more about
the little creature who had returned
it to her.

"**<u>Wait! Wait!</u>**" cried the frog. "Take me with you, I can't run as fast as you."

But what good did it do him to scream his "**<u>quark! quark!</u>**" after her as loud as he could? She wouldn't listen to him but hurried home where she soon forgot the poor frog, who now had to go back into his well again.

How would you feel if you were the frog?
(Circle your answer.)

MAD

EMBARRASSED

PUZZLED

SORRY FOR MYSELF

UNHAPPY

OTHER _____

_____

_____

12

The next evening, the Princess was eating her dinner at the royal table when—**plitch plotch, plitch plotch**—something came climbing up the stairs. When it reached the door, it knocked at the door and cried:

**Youngest daughter of the King,
Open the door for me!**

The Princess rose from the table and
ran to see who was calling her—when she
opened the door, there sat the frog,
wet and green and cold! Quickly she
slammed the door and sat down at the
table again, her heart beating loud
and fast. The King could see well enough
that she was frightened and worried,
and he said, "My child, what are you
afraid of? Is there a giant out there who
wants to carry you away?"

"Oh no," said the Princess. "It's not a
giant, but a horrid old frog!"

"And what does he want of you?"
asked the King.

"Oh, dear father, as I was playing
under the linden tree by the well,
my golden ball fell into the water.
And because I cried so hard, the frog
brought it back to me; and because

he insisted so much, I promised him that he could be my playmate. But I never, never thought that he would ever leave his well. Now he is out there and wants to come in and eat from my plate and drink from my cup and sleep in my little bed. But I couldn't bear that, papa, he's so wet and ugly and his eyes bulge out!"

While she was talking, the frog knocked at the door once more and said:

Youngest daughter of the King,
    Open the door for me.
Mind your words at the old well spring;
    Open the door for me!

At that the King said, "If we make promises, daughter, we must keep them; so you had better go and open the door."

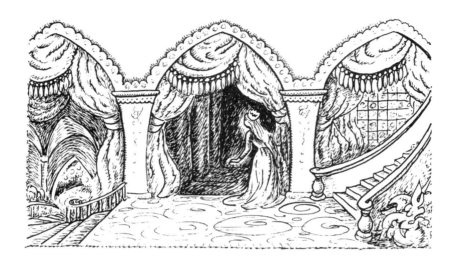

The Princess still did not want to
do it but she had to obey. When she
opened the door, the frog hopped in
and followed her until she reached
her chair. Then he sat there and said,
"Lift me up beside you."

She hesitated—the frog was so cold
and clammy—but her father looked at her
sternly and said, "You must keep your
promise."

After the frog was on her chair,
he wanted to be put on the table.
When he was there, he said, "Now shove
your plate a little closer, so we can eat
together like real playmates."

The Princess shuddered, but she had
to do it. The frog enjoyed the meal and
ate heartily, but the poor girl could not
swallow a single bite. At last the frog said,
"Now I've eaten enough and I feel tired.
Carry me to your room so I can go
to sleep."

The Princess began to cry. It had been
hard enough to touch the cold fat frog,
and worse still to have him eat out of her
plate, but to have him beside her in her
little bed was more than she could bear.

"I want to go to bed," repeated the
frog. "Take me there and tuck me in."

Do you think the
Princess should
have to keep
this promise?
(Circle your answer.)

 YES   NO

Why or why not?

The Princess shuddered again and looked at her father, but he only said, "He helped you in your trouble. Is it fair to scorn him now?"

There was nothing for her to do but to pick up the creature—she did it with two fingers—and to carry him up into her room, where she dropped him in a corner on the floor, hoping he would be satisfied. But after she had gone to bed, she heard something she didn't like. **Ploppety plop! Ploppety plop!** It was the frog hopping across the floor, and when he reached her bed he said, "I'm tired and the floor is too hard. I have as much right as you to sleep in a good soft bed. Lift me up or I will tell your father."

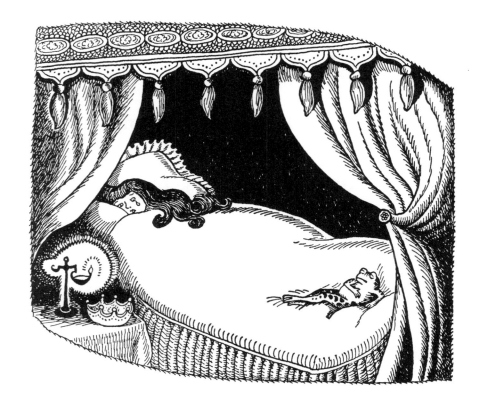

At this the Princess was bitterly angry
but she picked him up and put him at the
foot-end of her bed. There he stayed
all night but when the dark was greying
into daylight, the frog jumped down
from the bed, out of the door and away,
she knew not where.

The next night it was the same.
The frog came back, knocked at the door
and said:

> **Youngest daughter of the King,**
> **   Open the door for me.**
> **Mind your words at the old well spring;**
> **   Open the door for me!**

There was nothing for her to do but
let him in. Again he ate out of her golden
plate, sipped out of her golden cup,
and again he slept at the foot-end of her
bed. In the morning he went away
as before.

The third night he came again.
This time he was not content to sleep
at her feet.

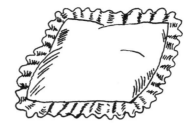

"I want to sleep under your pillow," he said. "I think I'd like it better there."

The girl thought she would never be able to sleep with a horrid, damp, goggle-eyed frog under her pillow. She began to weep softly to herself and couldn't stop until at last she cried herself to sleep.

When the night was over and the morning sunlight burst in at the window, the frog crept out from under her pillow and hopped off the bed. But as soon as his feet touched the floor something happened to him. In that moment he was no longer a cold, fat, goggle-eyed frog, but a young Prince with handsome friendly eyes!

Why is the spell over the frog broken even though the Princess isn't nice to him?

"You see," he said, "I wasn't what I seemed to be! A wicked old woman bewitched me. No one but you could break the spell, little Princess, and I waited and waited at the well for you to help me."

The Princess was speechless with surprise but her eyes sparkled.

"And will you let me be your playmate now?" said the Prince, laughing. "**Mind your words at the old well spring!**"

At this the Princess laughed too, and they both ran out to play with the golden ball.

For years they were the best of friends and the happiest of playmates, and it is not hard to guess, I'm sure, that when they were grown up they were married and lived happily ever after.

The Prince and the Princess Together

Would you like to have the Princess as your friend?

YES   NO

Why or why not? _____

_____

_____

_____

My Question

Name

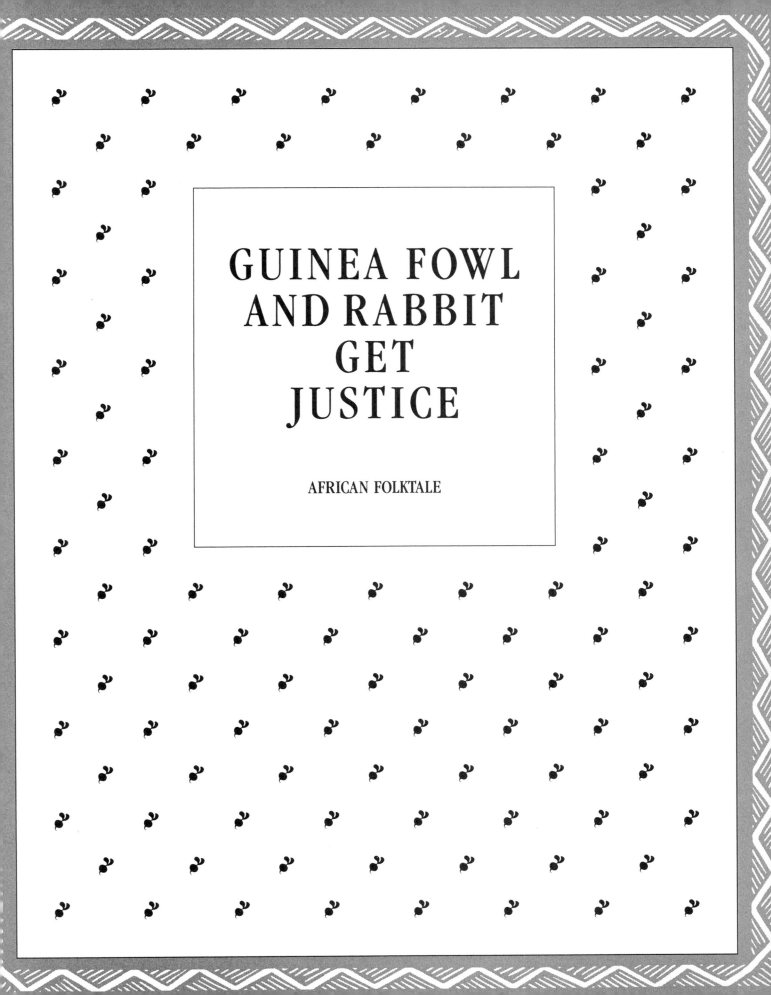

GUINEA FOWL AND RABBIT GET JUSTICE

AFRICAN FOLKTALE

My favorite trick is _____

Somewhere between the Kong Mountains and the sea, in the country called the Gold Coast, the bird named Guinea Fowl had his farm. It was a good farm. Guinea Fowl worked hard on it, and grew fine yams and bananas. He grew beans and okra, millet and tobacco. His farm always looked green and prosperous. Mostly it was because

Guinea Fowl was a hard worker. Not very far away Rabbit had a farm. It wasn't a very good farm because Rabbit never worked too hard. He planted at planting time, but he never hoed his crops or pulled out the weeds that grew there. So when harvest time came along there wasn't very much okra or beans or millet.

One day Rabbit was out walking and he saw Guinea Fowl's farm. It looked so much better than his own that he wished he owned it. He thought it over. He became indignant.

"Why is it that it rains over here on Guinea Fowl's land and not on mine, so that his crops grow and mine don't?" he asked himself. "**It's not fair!**"

Why does Rabbit think his farm should be as good as Guinea Fowl's, even though he does no work?

30

He thought all day. And a wonderful
idea came to him.

That night he brought out his wife
and his children and marched them
to Guinea Fowl's farm, then he marched
them back again. He did it again. All night
his family went back and forth from their
house to Guinea Fowl's farm, until by
morning they had made a trail. In the
morning they started pulling up Guinea
Fowl's vegetables and putting them
in baskets.

When Guinea Fowl came to work he
saw Rabbit there with his family, pulling
up all the fine crops he had planted.

"What are you doing with my yams
and okra?" Guinea Fowl said. "And what
are you doing on my farm, anyway?"

"*Your* farm?" Rabbit said. "There
must be some mistake. It's *my* farm."

"I guess there *is* a mistake. It's my farm.
I planted it and I weeded it and I
hoed it," Guinea Fowl said. "So I don't
see how it can be your farm."

"How could you plant it and weed it and hoe it when I planted it and weeded it and hoed it?" Rabbit said.

Guinea Fowl was very angry.

"**You'd better get off my place**," he said.

"**You'd better get off *my* place**," Rabbit said.

"It's absurd," Guinea Fowl said.

"It certainly is," Rabbit said, "when any old Guinea Fowl can come and claim someone else's property."

"**It's mine**," Guinea Fowl said.

"**It's mine**," Rabbit said.

"Well, I'll take the case to the chief," Guinea Fowl said.

"It's a good idea," Rabbit said.

So the two of them picked up their
hoes and went to the village to the house
of the chief.

"This fellow is pulling up my
vegetables," Guinea Fowl said, "and he
won't get off my farm."

"He's trying to take advantage of me,"
Rabbit said. "I work and work to grow
fine yams and then he comes along
and wants to own them."

They argued and argued, while the
head man listened. Finally they went
out together to look the situation over.

"Where is the trail from your house?" the head man asked Rabbit.

"There," Rabbit said, and pointed out the one he had just made.

"And where is the trail from your house?" the head man asked Guinea Fowl.

"Trail? I never had a trail," Guinea Fowl said.

"Whenever anyone has a farm he has a trail to it from his house," the head man said.

"But whenever I come to work my farm I *fly*," Guinea Fowl said.

The head man thought. He shook his head.

"If a person has a farm he has to have a trail to it," he said after a while. "So the land must belong to Rabbit."

He went away. Rabbit and his family began to pull up more yams. Guinea Fowl went home, feeling very angry.

When Rabbit had a large basket full of vegetables he started off to market with them. But the basket was very heavy. He wasn't used to heavy work, because he was lazy. After he had carried his load a little distance along the road he put it down to rest. And while he sat by the roadside Guinea Fowl came along.

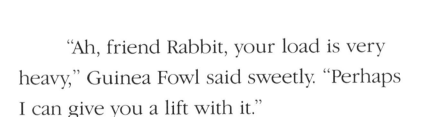

"Ah, friend Rabbit, your load is very heavy," Guinea Fowl said sweetly. "Perhaps I can give you a lift with it."

Rabbit was touched. Guinea Fowl wasn't angry any more. He was very friendly.

"Thank you," he said. "You are a real friend to help me with my vegetables."

Why does Rabbit believe Guinea Fowl is being a friend when Guinea Fowl offers to help him?

36

So Guinea Fowl put the load on his head. He smiled at Rabbit. Then he flapped his wings and went off with the load, not to the market but to his own house.

Rabbit shouted. He ran after Guinea Fowl, but he couldn't catch him. Guinea Fowl soared over the fields and was gone.

Rabbit was angry. He went back to the village to find the head man.

"Guinea Fowl has robbed me!" he shouted. "He flew away with my basket of vegetables!"

The head man sent for Guinea Fowl.

"They were my vegetables I took," Guinea Fowl said.

"They were mine," Rabbit shouted. "I harvested them with my own hands!"

They argued and argued. The head man thought and thought.

"Well," he said at last, "when people carry things a great deal on their heads, after a while the hair gets thin from so much carrying." The people of the village said yes, that always happened.

"Let me see the top of your head," the head man said to Rabbit.

Rabbit showed him. The head man clicked his tongue.

"No," he said to Rabbit, "your hair is thick and long."

He turned to Guinea Fowl.

"Let me see yours," he said, and Guinea Fowl showed him.

Guinea Fowl's head didn't have even a fuzzy feather on it.

"It must belong to you," the head man said, "you are absolutely bald."

"But Guinea Fowl never *had* any feathers on his head!" Rabbit complained. "He was *always* bald!"

"When you carry things on your head the hair becomes thin," the head man said. "So the basket belongs to Guinea Fowl."

They went away. Rabbit prepared another basket of vegetables to take to market. And when he set it down by the side of the road to rest, Guinea Fowl swooped down and took it away. Rabbit prepared another basket, and the same thing happened. It was no use going to the head man any more, because Guinea Fowl's head was so bald.

At last Rabbit got tired of pulling up Guinea Fowl's vegetables for him, and he went back to his own farm to work for himself.

That is why people sometimes say, "The shortest path often goes nowhere."

Do you think Rabbit will live differently now? (Circle your answer.)

YES   NO

Why or why not?

40

What is Rabbit doing on his farm? TAKEING
FOOD FROM HIM.

I think the head man is   wise

                                 silly

because _____

_____

_____

42

My Question

_____

_____

_____

_____

Name _____

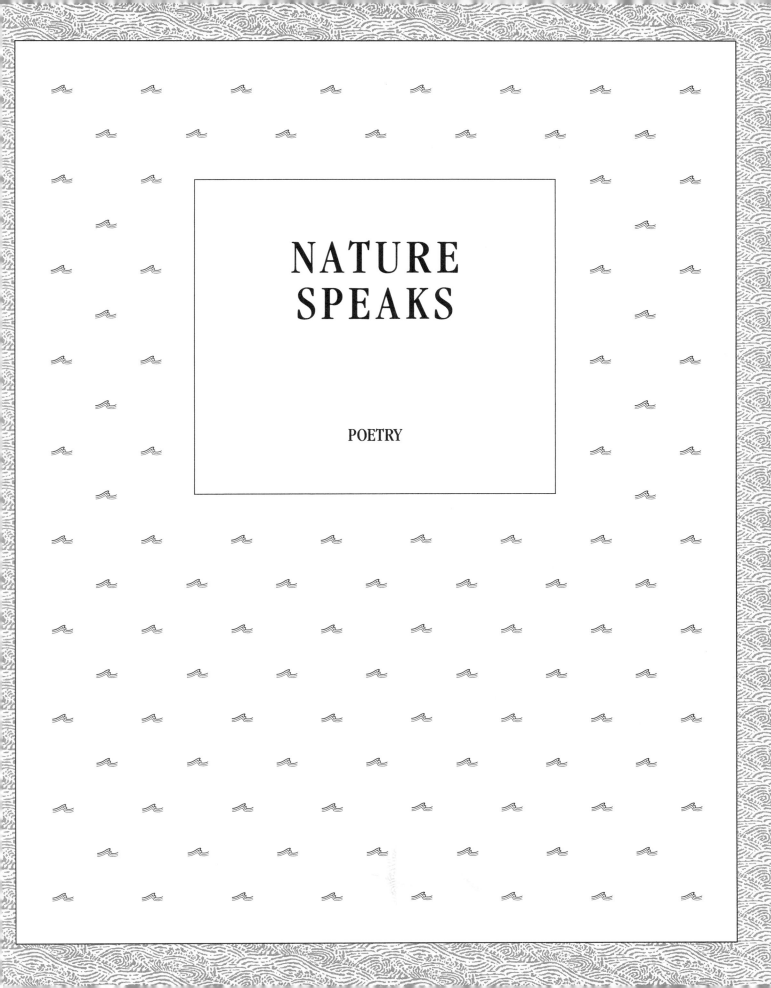

NATURE SPEAKS

POETRY

THEME IN YELLOW

I spot the hills
With yellow balls in autumn.
I light the prairie cornfields
Orange and tawny gold clusters
And I am called pumpkins.

Why is the pumpkin proud that it can color the world around it?

On the last of October

When dusk is fallen

Children join hands

And circle round me

Singing ghost songs

And love to the harvest moon;

How do the children feel when they dance around the jack-o'-lantern?

I am a jack-o'-lantern
With terrible teeth
And the children know
I am fooling.

—Carl Sandburg

Why do the children know that the jack-o'-lantern is only fooling?

48

The Last of October

Theme in Red

I _AM A MAN WHO IS ALL RED AND_

I am called _THE MAN WHO CAN MAKE ANYthing RED_

50

My Question

_____

_____

_____

Name _____

THE WIND

I can get through a doorway without any key,
And strip the leaves from the great oak tree.

I can drive storm-clouds and shake tall towers,
Or steal through a garden and not wake the flowers.

Seas I can move and ships I can sink;
I can carry a house-top or the scent of a pink.

When I am angry I can rave and riot;
And when I am spent, **I lie quiet as quiet.**

—James Reeves

AIR

+ TORNADO

I like the wind best when it is

strong

gentle

I DONT LIKE THE WIND WHEN IT IS

SEASHELL

They've brought me a seashell.

Inside it sings
a map of the sea.
My heart
fills up with water,
with smallish fish
of shade and silver.

They've brought me a seashell.

—**Federico García Lorca**
(translated by K. F. Pearson)

CARACOLA

Me han traído una caracola.

Dentro le canta
un mar de mapa.
Mi corazón
se llena de agua,
con pececillos
de sombra y plata.

Me han traído una caracola.

—Federico García Lorca

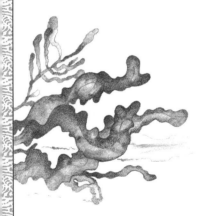

A Map of the Sea

My Favorite Words

Acknowledgments

—

All possible care has been taken to trace ownership and secure permission for each selection in this series. The Great Books Foundation wishes to thank the following authors, publishers, and representatives for permission to reprint the copyrighted material in this volume:

The Frog Prince, from TALES FROM GRIMM, by Jacob and Wilhelm Grimm, freely translated and illustrated by Wanda Gág. Copyright 1936 by Wanda Gág; renewed 1964 by Robert Janssen. Reprinted by permission of Coward, McCann & Geoghegan.

Guinea Fowl and Rabbit Get Justice, from THE COW-TAIL SWITCH AND OTHER WEST AFRICAN STORIES, by Harold Courlander and George Herzog. Copyright 1947 by Henry Holt and Company, Inc. Copyright 1975 by Harold Courlander and George Herzog. Copyright 1986 by Harold Courlander. Reprinted by permission of Harold Courlander.

"Theme in Yellow," from CHICAGO POEMS, by Carl Sandburg. Copyright 1916 by Holt, Rinehart and Winston, Inc.; renewed 1944 by Carl Sandburg. Reprinted by permission of Harcourt Brace Jovanovich, Inc.

"The Wind," from THE WANDERING MOON AND OTHER POEMS, by James Reeves. Copyright 1987 by James Reeves. Reprinted by permission of the James Reeves Estate.

"Seashell," by Federico García Lorca, translated by K. F. Pearson, from MESSAGES OF THINGS, by K. F. Pearson. Copyright 1984 by K. F. Pearson. Reprinted by permission of K. F. Pearson.

Illustration Credits

—

Wanda Gág's illustrations for *The Frog Prince* are from TALES FROM GRIMM and MORE TALES FROM GRIMM (copyright 1947 by the Wanda Gág Estate; renewed 1974 by Robert Janssen). Reprinted by permission of Coward-McCann. Reproduced with permission from original illustrations and first editions in the Children's Literature Research Collection, University of Minnesota. Illustrations on pages 20 and 21 by William Seabright.

Patti Green prepared the illustrations for *Guinea Fowl and Rabbit Get Justice*.

David Cunningham prepared the illustrations for *"Theme in Yellow."*

Jorge Colombo prepared the illustrations for *"The Wind."*

William Seabright prepared the illustrations for *"Seashell."*

"G.B." was created by Ed Young. Copyright 1990 by Ed Young.

Cover art by David Frampton.

Cover and book design by William Seabright and Paul Uhl, Design Associates.